HIDDEN TREASURES

OMAGH

Edited by Sarah Andrew

First published in Great Britain in 2002 by
YOUNG WRITERS
Remus House,
Coltsfoot Drive,
Peterborough, PE2 9JX
Telephone (01733) 890066

Copyright Contributors 2002

HB ISBN 0 75433 828 2
SB ISBN 0 75433 829 0

FOREWORD

This year, the Young Writers' Hidden Treasures competition proudly presents a showcase of the best poetic talent from over 72,000 up-and-coming writers nationwide.

Young Writers was established in 1991 and we are still successful, even in today's technologically-led world, in promoting and encouraging the reading and writing of poetry.

The thought, effort, imagination and hard work put into each poem impressed us all, and once again, the task of selecting poems was a difficult one, but nevertheless, an enjoyable experience.

We hope you are as pleased as we are with the final selection and that you and your family continue to be entertained with *Hidden Treasures Omagh* for many years to come.

CONTENTS

Gortin Primary School

Avril Ballantine	1
Alan Nesbitt	2
Jessica Baxter	3
Jason Fleming	4
Amy Godber	5
Adam McFarland	6
Bryony Houston	7
Gareth Kennedy	8
Lauren McFarland	9
Lisa McFarland	10
Mark Scott	11
Kyle McIlwaine	12
Rachel McKelvey	13
Adam Fleming	14
Sarah-Louise Campbell	15
Kyra Campbell	16
Aaron Campbell	17
Ashley Whelan	18
Jonathan Campbell	19
Andrew Baxter	20

Langfield Primary School

Zara-Jayne McCauley	21
Leanne Long	22
Zara Bogle	23
Chloe Kerr	24
Ashley McCauley	25
Wendy Liggett	26
Lee McClelland	27
Gemma Harkin	28
Tracy Liggett	29
Gary McClelland	30

Loreto Convent Primary School

Rebecca Johnston	31
Emma O'Sullivan	32
Laura Donnelly	33
Margaret Coll	34
Louise Sweeney	35
Danielle Drumm	36
Grainne McNabb	37
Shauna McGurk	38
Lucy Garrity	39
Laura Smyth	40
Sandra McCrory	41
Chloe Loughrey	42
Jade Campbell	43
Teresa McClean	44
Shannon Maclennan	45
Naomi McLarnon	46
Laura Maguire	47
Edel McMahon	48
Niamh Simmonds	49
Fiona McGoldrick	50
Nicôle Townsend	51
Niamh Meyler	52
Essie-May Sharkey	53
Sarah Baxter	54
Orla Fox	55

Omagh Integrated Primary School

Year 2	56
Shauna Mulligan	57
Aódhan Donnelly	58
Leanne Stark	59
Kieran McCusker	60
Michael Laverty	61
Matthew Smyth	62
Kirstie Colhoun	63
Mark Garrity	64
Chloe-Beth Acheson	65

Andre Sturm	66
James Mitchell	67
Art Cook	68
Peter Donnelly	69
Alex McKinley	70
Niamh Slane	71
Richard Bradley	72
Stephanie McGuckin	73
Grainne Hand	74
Emma O'Shea	75
Gavin Scott	76
Steven McCusker	77
Melissa Smith	78
Josiah Whitworth	79
Patrick Grant	80
Ieuan Maguire	81
Paul McCrystal	82
Paul Campbell	83
Sarah Crawford	84

Roscavey Primary School

Fearghal McMahon	85
Antonnia Susan Reid	86
Patrick Donnelly	87
Shauneen Smyth	88
Roisin McSorley	89
Caroline McNelis	90
Samone Ann Reid	91
Kerry McNelis	92
Michelle Woods	93
Anita McSorley	94
Cathy Donnelly	95

St Colmcille's Primary School

Michael Lynn	96
Cathal Byrne	97
Ryan McBride	98
Martin Lilly	99

John Maguire	100
Justin Blanchard	101
Joseph McDermott	102
Ryan Hackett	103
Rory Breslin	104
Richard Chism	106
Conor Madden	107
Ciaran O'Doherty	108
Peter Harte	109
Michael Sharkey	110

St Macartan's Primary School

Aine Maguire	111
Cathan McCourt	112
Ciaran Slevin	113
Sean Curran	114

St Mary's Primary School

Donna McManus	115
Lauren McRory	116
Sarah Murray	117
Roisin Brogan	118
Laura Harper	119
Ciara McGartland	120
Nicole Ward	121
Callum McKinney	122
Ciara Kelly	123
Melissa McDonagh	124
Andrew McDowell	125
Colleen Owens	126
Naoise Devlin	127
Moira Fox	128
Sinead Morris	129
Seamus Slevin	130
Shona McAleer	131
Cahir McKenny	132
Samantha Munton	134

St Peter's Primary School

Amanda Hood	135
Rosaleen Bradley	136
Nuala Kelly	137
Mark Sharkey	138
Carmel McBride	139
Adrian McBride	140
Ciara Furey	141
Denise McCullagh	142
Orla Harkin	143
Beth Donnelly	144
Catherine Morris	145
Michael McCullagh	146
Eilis Kearney	147
Mark McDermott	148
Danielle McGaughey	149
Brendan Kelly	150
Colm Hicks	151
Brigid McCullagh	152
Patricia Morris	153
Jamie Allen	154
Gerard McBride	155
Niamh Murphy	156
Shane McBride	157
Piaras Bradley	158
Aine Conway	159

St Teresa's Primary School

Kevin Ward	160
Niall Donaghy	161
Conor Donnelly	162
Kellie Boyle	163
Peter Grugan	164
Niamh McElduff	165
Mairéad Kelly	166
Bronagh McAteer	167
Ryan Donaghy	168
Meadhbh O'Goan	169

Maire Gallagher	170
Aoife McElduff	171
Clodagh Donaghy	172
Sorcha Kelly	173
Helen Conway	174
Gráinne Moxon	175
Finbarr McElhatton	176
Noelle Kelly	177
Declan Grimes	178
Emily Donaghy	179
Niall McKernan	180
Donna Grimes	181
Conall Daly	182
Caryn Ward	183
Paula Kelly	184
Aidan McCullagh	185
Orla McCartan	186
Ciara McElduff	187
Sean McDermott	188

The Poems

FOXES

Foxes are covered with soft and cuddly fur,
They move very slowly,
They stretch as well,
They hunt for food and eat all kind of animals,
Foxes do not like anybody touching them,
So be careful.
If you see a fox, run away if you care,
So watch out or you will be in danger.

Avril Ballantine (9)
Gortin Primary School

BEAR

I am a bear and I have brown fur from head to toe,
I am a bear and I am very fierce,
I am a bear and I hate humans,
I am a bear and I like to scare humans.

Alan Nesbitt (8)
Gortin Primary School

GIRAFFE

I am a giraffe,
You see me in the zoo.
You can come to tea
With me if you want me to.
I have leaves and water for tea.
We can play,
You catch me.

Jessica Baxter (8)
Gortin Primary School

LION

L is for lions that pounce,
I is for insects that lions hate,.
O is for orange, the colour of its fur,
N is for noise when the lion roars.

Jason Fleming (8)
Gortin Primary School

TIGER

I am a tiger,
I am orange with black stripes,
I like meat and I want to eat you,
I like to jump and run about,
I am cuddly and soft with
a long tail like a cat.
My favourite thing is to catch animals
and *you* for my dinner.

Amy Godber (8)
Gortin Primary School

LION

I am a lion,
I have very sharp teeth,
I have an orange coat,
I eat zebras and antelopes,
First I lie in the tall grass and when they are eating,
I pounce on them and gobble them up.

Adam McFarland (9)
Gortin Primary School

WOODLOUSE

Woodlouse eating long grass and fat juicy leaves
Crawls on the ground like small stones blown by the wind.
Eventually dusk has come, time to crawl back under the brick.

Bryony Houston (9)
Gortin Primary School

RAINFORESTS

Rainforests rainforests
Are always damp and never cold.

Sometimes when there is rain
In the end it turns to steam.

There are some trees that are small
And some are very tall.
Also some are in-between.

Gareth Kennedy (10)
Gortin Primary School

TREES

T rees give us beauty.
R elax and play around them.
E njoy the wonderful scenery.
E arth is their wonderful home.
S ee the beauty in trees.

Lauren McFarland (9)
Gortin Primary School

MONKEYS

There were five little monkeys all on their own,
One saw an apple and then there were four.
Four little monkeys all on their own,
One went to play and then there were three.
Three little monkeys all on their own,
One went to the loo and then there were two.
Two little monkeys all on their own,
One went on the big dipper and then there was one.
That one was sad and went to bed.

Lisa McFarland (8)
Gortin Primary School

TREES

Trees are good for the environment.
Rangers look after the trees.
Evergreen trees are always green
Every day they are the same.
Streams run below the trees.

Trees clean the air.
Rabbits enjoy the trees.
Evergreen trees are tall.
Everyone enjoys trees.
Squirrels live in the trees.

Mark Scott (11)
Gortin Primary School

TREES

Hello, I am Mr Oaky
I'm a tree; I have lots of eyes.
I lose my hair in winter.
I hate that Woody Woodpecker,
Always pecking at my body.
My friend is Ash Bark.
One day a squirrel ran around my body,
He hid some nuts at my feet.
I look forward to him coming back.

Kyle McIlwaine (9)
Gortin Primary School

CATERPILLAR

A caterpillar crawls
It slithers up walls
Eating juicy leaves
It is as long as a snake
It wraps up into a cocoon shell
It changes into a butterfly
The butterfly flies up into the air
Up up and away.

Rachel McKelvey (9)
Gortin Primary School

MY BOOMERANG

Once I had a boomerang
I threw it over the road
It landed in the pond
And killed a poor wee toad

Once I had a boomerang
And I sent it flyin'
It went over Africa
And left a lion cryin'

Once I had a boomerang
I threw it out to sea
But I threw it too hard
It never came back to me.

Adam Fleming (9)
Gortin Primary School

Trees

T   rees beautiful things
R   elaxing places they give
E   conomics we get money from trees
E   arth's lungs producing oxygen
S   o important to animals.

Sarah-Louise Campbell (9)
Gortin Primary School

TREES

D   elicious fruits on trees
E   veryone appreciates trees
C   arbon dioxide swallowed up
I   nspiration for poets and artists
D   iverse animals live in trees
U   seful are trees for timber
O   ver the hills and far away the trees like night and day
U   nder the ground trees have roots
S   o to enable the tree to stand upright.

Kyra Campbell (10)
Gortin Primary School

TREES

I am a tree,
I stand tall in the forest
My hair is green,
I have loads of arms,
I hate monkeys
Because they swing on my body,
I hate fire because it
Burns my arms and fingers,
My body is made of wood
I hate humans
Because they cut me down,
My feet are deep
Deep in the ground.

Aaron Campbell (9)
Gortin Primary School

TREES

I am a tree
I am called Barkey
My hair is green
I have lots of arms
I hate woodpeckers
Woody is the worst
I am shelter for the squirrels
They store their nuts in my hair
I am very tall
I have lots of company in the forest.

Ashley Whelan (10)
Gortin Primary School

WORMS

Crawls along
Under the ground
Slimy wiggling
Long and brown.

Thin as a pin
As fat as a rat
I wonder does it
Wear a hat?

Jonathan Campbell (10)
Gortin Primary School

TREES

I am a tree
I hate baboons
They snap my arms
My hair is green
I have big eyes
I hate cats too because they steal my arms
And scratch my bark
I stand out tall in the forest
I don't like Mr Pecker because
He makes his home in my body.

Andrew Baxter (10)
Gortin Primary School

MY CAT

Spitter is his name,
Spitting is his game,
But now he is older,
He is even bolder.

I love my cat,
Even if he ate a rat.
Sometimes he smells,
And everyone tells
Him to get out.

Some people even call,
Spitter here's your ball!

Zara-Jayne McCauley (9)
Langfield Primary School

MY FRIEND

M y best friend is Leanne Davis,
Y ellow is the colour of her T-shirt,

F iona is her auntie,
R achel is her friend as well,
I an is her bigger brother,
E velyn is her granny as well,
N ever do we fight
D ays we go to each other's houses.

Leanne Long (10)
Langfield Primary School

FRIENDS

Zara Jayne is my best friend,
Friend for life,
Lifetime of fun,
Fun and secrets,
Secrets that no one else can share,
Share friendship and lots, lots more,
More fun than ever before.

Zara Bogle (9)
Langfield Primary School

PANDAS

Pandas have a diet of bamboo,
But they don't always get it at the zoo,
They mainly live in China but there are only 1000 left in the wild,
Newborns are smaller than a human newborn child,
At least they are protected by the Chinese law,
The great cuddly panda and his giant paw.

Chloe Kerr (9)
Langfield Primary School

VOLCANOES

Volcanoes
Have lava
Inside and when
They explode it is
A big surprise, people can
Get burned *alive* because of the
Liquid inside, people run as fast as
They can to get away from the red
Hot sand. The lava can be boiling bright red,
But if you get too close you'll sure be dead.

Ashley McCauley (10)
Langfield Primary School

LAMBS

The little lambs and their mummy ewes in the field,
Sipping up the water out of the drinker.
Eating the green grass and the buttercups.
Little tails wagging.
Skipping here and there.

Wendy Liggett (7)
Langfield Primary School

MY DOG CALLED SPOT

S   pot is black and white, he is a sheepdog with bright eyes.
P   at him hard and 'Ouch!' you'll go
O   ld he is but fast he goes through fields after sheep
T   ail waggles when I come home.

Lee McClelland (10)
Langfield Primary School

SPRINGTIME

S   pring is coming soon,
P   urpley flowers everywhere,
R   ain keeps them growing more every day,
I   ce kills the flowers and ice is slippy,
N   ew flowers always come every springtime,
G   rowing flowers are nice.

Gemma Harkin (10)
Langfield Primary School

MY DOGS

I have a dog called Spot,
and she is always hot,
she loves water,
she's like an otter,
and we love her a lot.

I have a dog called Duke,
everywhere he goes he likes to look,
sometimes he's bad
and Karen goes *mad*!
And everyone starts to look.

Tracy Liggett (9)
Langfield Primary School

RABBITS

R   abbits are cute,
A   rabbit can jump high,
B   unnies like to eat carrots,
B   unnies' tails bobbing,
I   t is black and white,
T   wo big ears twitching,
S   oft and cuddly.

Gary McClelland (8)
Langfield Primary School

MY BEST FRIEND

My best friend is Laura,
We love to play and run
In the spring showers.
When summer comes
We have such fun
Especially in the sun.
In autumn we jump in the leaves,
We bake cakes and buns
And wait until they're done
Then eat them up in our tums . . .
When winter comes around,
We play in the snow,
We build a jolly snowman
And have snowball fights.

Rebecca Johnston (9)
Loreto Convent Primary School

My Cat

I have a little cat
and she is very fat.
She eats an awful lot
of Kit-e-kat.
She's a very happy cat
and she purrs quite a lot
when she sees me every day.
She's a very fluffy cat
and she wags her tail.
I love my black and white cat.

Emma O'Sullivan (8)
Loreto Convent Primary School

MY FRIEND

My friend is called Rebecca
She has beautiful blonde hair and deep blue eyes.
Her sister's called Hannah
But she has no brothers.
We love to play
On long sunny days.
We share our secrets
And go to the cinema together.
Rebecca is really
A great friend to have.

Laura Donnelly (8)
Loreto Convent Primary School

MY SKATEBOARD

I love to go on my skateboard
But I don't like to fall,
I love to go on my skateboard
Instead of playing ball.
It's hard to go on a skateboard
When you're only three feet tall,
But I love my skateboard
Even when I hit the wall!

Margaret Coll (9)
Loreto Convent Primary School

TRAGEDY

It was a shock to me, at half-past three,
One Tuesday in September.
When I heard the news, I was confused.
People were hurt and buildings were burnt.
Some people died and we all cried,
While others jumped from buildings.
Why this happened - we don't know
But that day never from my mind will go,
That tragic day in September.

Louise Sweeney (11)
Loreto Convent Primary School

SEPTEMBER 11TH 2001

It was such an awful tragedy,
It hurt the whole society,
Two planes crashed,
Made the buildings smash.
President Bush was so mad,
And the whole of the world is so sad,
The Twin Towers will always
Be in our hearts
But now they're lying
In bits and parts.

Danielle Drumm (11)
Loreto Convent Primary School

SPRING

The spring comes once a year.
It makes us happy and makes us cheer.
The flowers start to bloom and
Everywhere does not look so full of gloom.
The little lambs start to play.
The farmers are busy preparing the hay.

Grainne McNabb (8)
Loreto Convent Primary School

SPRING

Spring is a wonderful time of year,
When new life begins to appear,
There are tiny buds on the trees,
And little lambs skipping in the breeze,
Birds are busy building nests,
But the cuckoo takes a rest.

Children play in the sun,
And they have brilliant fun,
The flowers are growing,
And the wind is blowing gently.

Shauna McGurk (9)
Loreto Convent Primary School

MY SISTER

I have got a baby sister,
She is two years old,
Sometimes she is good,
Sometimes she is bold,
She likes me to read at bedtime,
Her favourite story is Goldilocks,
And she likes poems that rhyme,
Even though she is hard work
For my family and me,
I love my sister Moya,
She is the whole world to me.

Lucy Garrity (9)
Loreto Convent Primary School

SUMMERTIME

I can't wait until summer,
I will get out to run,
And have plenty of fun,
The sun will shine,
On the clothes on the line,
And I will feel fine,
Because it's the summer holiday.

Laura Smyth (9)
Loreto Convent Primary School

THE FOUR SEASONS

Spring is when the lambs and bulbs appear.
The good weather is here.

Summer at last, the blazing sun.
Sand and sea for everyone.

Autumn leaves fall to the ground, yellow, orange and brown.
All these colours can be found.

Winter, the coldest of all the seasons.
Wrap up warm before it freezes.

Sandra McCrory (9)
Loreto Convent Primary School

SPRING

I love the springtime
The evenings are bright,
It takes a wee bit longer
To get to night.
The springtime is great
For flowering buds
That rise from their beds
From a winter's sleep.
The young spring lambs hop
Around the fields
Their first taste of freedom
From their mothers' bay.
Though the springtime is great
It's the opening gate
To the warm summer months
When the holidays are great.

Chloe Loughrey (9)
Loreto Convent Primary School

THE JOYS OF WINTER

Sitting here watching the Christmas delights,
Seeing children playing,
Building snowmen and having snowball fights,
Christmas morning comes early,
Opening presents and having fun,
Sitting with my baby sister, my mum and dad,
Going to mass and saying prayers,
Seeing family and all of my friends,
Having dinner at the table and having so much fun,
So I just can't wait for next year to come!

Jade Campbell (9)
Loreto Convent Primary School

CHRISTMAS

Christmas is a celebration
A beautiful time of year,
As we wait for Father Christmas
I'm just glad it's near.
Little robin redbreast
Is the best,
He reminds me of Christmas
And all the rest.
The fairy lights on the tree
Bring happy memories back to me.
The turkey roasting in the oven,
The log on the fire
Fills my heart
With sweet desire.
The carol singers here and there
Doing all they can
Giving a helping hand.
But for me, the sound I like to hear
Is very, very near,
Sleigh bells ringing,
Santa singing, ho, ho, ho!

Teresa McClean (8)
Loreto Convent Primary School

A Spring Poem

I love spring because
Fancy flowers rise up,
Little lambs are born,
Busy birds make their nests
While rattling rain takes a rest,
Before you know it, it's Easter time,
And all around, new life begins.

Shannon Maclennan (8)
Loreto Convent Primary School

THE SEASONS

Spring is when the bluebirds sing,
Lambs' fleeces are white as snow,
Baby birds try to fly high in the sky,
The smell of fresh grass and the song of the birds,
Spring is everywhere.

The summery days of summer are beautiful every day,
The sunshine shines through the rain,
Casting rainbows beyond the rainy sky,
Sunny days the children come out to play.

Autumn we will come and scatter all the leaves,
And rake them all up again,
Back from summer holidays,
Back to school again.

Winter comes and best of all,
Santa knocks on my door,
Time for all the stockings to be put on the wall,
And for the Christmas tree, ever so tall,
That is all my seasons that I have to say,
I really should be on my way,
Have a lovely day.

Naomi McLarnon (8)
Loreto Convent Primary School

CHRISTMAS

Christmas is the best time for boys and girls to play
They have lots of fun on Christmas day.
They build snowmen made out of snow,
Until it is time for them to go.
Santa comes on Christmas eve,
Only to children who believe.
Christmas is the time when Jesus was born,
On a quiet Christmas morn.

Laura Maguire (8)
Loreto Convent Primary School

SPRING

S   is for the sky which will be blue from March to July.
P   is for petals that appear on flowers.
R   is for the robin which isn't far away.
I   is for insects that crawl from under the stones.
N   is for no more dark evenings.
G   is for the grass starts to grow again.

Edel McMahon (8)
Loreto Convent Primary School

CHRISTMAS

Christmas is a time of joy when baby Jesus was born.
We go to mass on Christmas morn to celebrate the birth.
After mass we have our dinner,
Turkey, ham and roast potatoes with all the trimmings.
On the night before a very special man appears
When we are in bed and fast asleep.
He leaves us gifts galore.
Can you guess who this special man is?
Of course, it's Santa Claus whom we all adore.

Niamh Simmonds (9)
Loreto Convent Primary School

WINTER

Winter is the time when it snows
and when the strong wind blows,
wrap up warm because everyone knows
you get cold hands, cold cheeks and cold toes.
Build a snowman with big eyes
as the snow is falling from the skies,
and at night when it gets heavier
we go to bed,
wrap up in the cosy bedcovers.

Fiona McGoldrick (9)
Loreto Convent Primary School

SPRING

Spring is here,
We all give a cheer,
The evenings are bright,
Which is such a delight.

All the snowdrops showing,
And daffodils growing,
Little lambs are bleating,
Mothers and their babies are meeting.

Lovely glittering ponies' coats,
And fresh milk from the goats,
The gleaming sun,
And all the children are having great fun.

Buds are appearing on the trees,
There are black and yellow bumblebees,
Lots of colourful butterflies,
And raindrops shining in the sky.

Nicôle Townsend (8)
Loreto Convent Primary School

SPRING

When I look out my window,
I see the daffodils beginning to grow,
I like to see the buds on trees,
When I stand in the cool breeze.

The mornings are getting brighter,
And the birds are singing in the trees,
I know now that spring has come,
The lambs and calves are born.

Niamh Meyler (8)
Loreto Convent Primary School

NETBALL, NETBALL

We play netball after school
With Siobhan our coach, who's really cool.
She doesn't shout or get cross,
But lets us know that she's the boss.
We sometimes win and sometimes lose,
We run hard and try to score.
Ducking and diving until we're sore,
We try to jump very high
And sometimes the ball hits the sky.
I like to run and catch the ball,
And hope and pray that I don't fall.

Essie-May Sharkey (8)
Loreto Convent Primary School

SPRING IS . . .

Little lambs,
Bursting buds,
Easter eggs,
Busy birds,
Sun shining,
Beautiful bluebells,
Tall tulips,
Snowy snowdrops,
Different daffodils.

Sarah Baxter (9)
Loreto Convent Primary School

MY CAT

My cat is four years old
He is good but sometimes bold.
His name is Pat
But he answers to more than that.
He likes to sit by the fire.
He plays in the fields
And gets stuck in the wire.
I have to go and help him out
But sometimes I get cross
And scream and shout.
He is my best friend
Without a doubt.
I would miss him loads
If he wasn't about.

Orla Fox (8)
Loreto Convent Primary School

ROBBER RED

Robber Red is naughty.
He climbs into a house.
He steals lots of things
And leaves as quiet as a mouse.

Robber Red is a rascal.
He wears lots of red.
He has a stack of stolen goods
And hides them under his bed.

Year 2
Omagh Integrated Primary School

HAY FEVER

Hay fever comes, grass now short.
Rub your eye and you get caught.
Stuck with black, you can't see
Another attack from hay fever.

Hay fever comes, no grass for you.
Sit on concrete or get the flu.
Don't go near hay or grass unless
You want the hay fever stress.

Shauna Mulligan (9)
Omagh Integrated Primary School

SPRING

One day I saw a daffodil going to grow
But it was a little low.
One day I saw some snowdrops,
That was a wonderful sight,
But a little bit white.

Aódhan Donnelly (8)
Omagh Integrated Primary School

MRS WITCH

There once was a witch,
Who lived in a ditch,
And to tell you the truth,
She was very rich.

She became very hairy,
And got very scary,
So she had to change her name,
To little Aunt Mary.

She quit being a witch,
And got a new job,
And became Big Bob.
She was so hairy,
That nobody could tell,
She once was a witch that cast nasty spells.

Leanne Stark (10)
Omagh Integrated Primary School

FEAR

My worst fear
Is when I just peer
Right over a cliff
And the waves splash
Onto the rocky shore
And you just wish there was a floor
And a door
So that you can get away
From near death.

Kieran McCusker (12)
Omagh Integrated Primary School

SANDWICH FOR LUNCH

I want something new for a change,
And I'll need something top of the range,
I wonder what I should do,
Maybe I should make some stew,
Nah!

I'll butter two giant pieces of bread,
And cover it with a sauce coloured red,
I'll add some jam and some ham,
And maybe some peas and cheese.

Ninety meatballs all very small,
A big burst ball,
Add some pepperoni,
And some cannelloni.

I wonder if I will eat this,
Or give some to my friends,
Maybe I won't give it away,
Only if they pay.

Michael Laverty (10)
Omagh Integrated Primary School

JAM SANDWICH

I want to have brunch
Instead of lunch.
A sandwich or two or even three
It will have to be!
Green jam, purple ham
Lots of red jam
All over the ham
And some small meatballs
This big, this big
As big as
You.

Matthew Smyth (11)
Omagh Integrated Primary School

KIRSTIE UP THE TREE

I was walking in the park one day
When I saw a great big tree,
Soon was I to find out
It was a Gummerrumma tree.

I looked up at the highest branch
And what was I to see?
A great big elephant
Looking down at me.

I asked him why he was up there,
He said he was chased,
I asked by whom,
'I was chased by a hunter,' he said.

I went to get a ladder,
'I'll be back soon,' I said,
I laid the ladder against the tree
And started to climb up high.

I got up to the elephant,
And told him to jump down,
Then the ladder, it fell down,
Now I am up the tree.

Kirstie Colhoun (11)
Omagh Integrated Primary School

HOW ABSURD

Put ham and jam,
Put mustard and custard,
Put salmon and lemon,
Put cheese and peas,
And plenty of butter please,
Give me food or
I will be very rude.

Mark Garrity (11)
Omagh Integrated Primary School

ANGER

Anger is red
It tastes like hot pepperoni
Anger smells like a burning fire
Anger looks like an erupting volcano
It sounds like a gunshot
Anger feels like pulling my hair
Anger is a hot meal at night
Making you choke.

Chloe-Beth Acheson (10)
Omagh Integrated Primary School

AUTUMN

Brown leaves fall off trees,
Animals hibernate,
Birds migrate,
Trees sleep for winter.

Nights get longer, days get shorter,
Weather gets colder and wetter,
Hallowe'en holidays are great,
Then we can hibernate.

Andre Sturm (9)
Omagh Integrated Primary School

FACES

Round faces, short faces,
Big faces, small faces.
Faces that are happy,
Faces that are sad,
Faces that are cross,
Faces that are mad.
Faces that are angry,
Faces that are scary,
Faces that are cheery,
Faces that are weary.
Faces with freckles,
Faces with spots.
Faces that are old,
Faces that are young,
Faces that are small,
Faces that are long.
Pale faces,
Dark faces,
All different faces looking at me.

James Mitchell (8)
Omagh Integrated Primary School

MY MOUTH

I like my mouth,
It talks when I want to,
And it helps me chew.
It bites when I'm eating,
And argues when I'm competing.
My mouth laughs like a hyena,
It also drinks Ribena.
My mouth can shout,
Out and about.
My mouth whispers,
Messages to Christopher,
My mouth can sing,
As good as a king.

Art Cook (9)
Omagh Integrated Primary School

THE SANDWICH

I want something different for my lunch,
I'll make up something for my brunch.
I'll need something saucy,
I'll need something glossy.
I'll pile on the pastrami,
Oh and some salami.
I'll put on some nacho cheese,
No! Can't take that, it makes me sneeze!
I'll put in some wine,
That looks just fine.
I'll put in some berries,
Add in some sherry.
All it needs is some honey,
Then I'll sell it for lots of money.

Peter Donnelly (11)
Omagh Integrated Primary School

RAINBOW

Red, yellow and pink,
It makes me really blink.
Red, yellow, pink and green,
It really makes a scene.
Red, green, pink and yellow,
It really is a happy fellow.

Alex McKinley (8)
Omagh Integrated Primary School

HOW TO MAKE A JAM SANDWICH FOR A GIANT

To make a giant a jam sandwich,
You have to have some bread,
And you have to have a lot of jam,
Nice, yummy and red.

This sandwich should be really big,
Probably as big as you,
But don't ever, ever think of having a chew,
Because the giant will be really cross with you!

Niamh Slane (11)
Omagh Integrated Primary School

CROCODILE

One day I was walking in the park.
I saw a fully grown crocodile.
It came out of the pond and swallowed a duck.
I was nearly opposite the crocodile.
Then it came over to me,
I started to run away.
It chased me along the path,
It followed me up a tree.
Now I have to end the poem,
It gets too gruesome
For all you little children.

Richard Bradley (11)
Omagh Integrated Primary School

EARS

Ears can hear people speak.
They can hear the traffic beep,
Or hear the wind late at night.
They don't bring tears.
Ears that are big,
Ears that are small,
Ears can hear when I call.
Ears, ears can hear
A lot of things,
Ears.

Stephanie McGuckin (8)
Omagh Integrated Primary School

FEET

Feet that are big,
Feet that are small,
Feet that are short,
Feet that are tall.
Feet with toes,
All neatly in rows,
Feet that wrinkle,
And toes that crinkle.
Feet that are broad,
Feet that are slim,
With their little toes
Around the rim.

Grainne Hand (9)
Omagh Integrated Primary School

HAIR

Hair that is short,
Hair that is long,
Hair that is black,
Hair that is brown,
Hair that is curly,
Hair that is straight.
Hair in a bun,
Hair just for fun.
Hair that is in a plait,
Hair in a matt.
I love my hair and that's that.

Emma O'Shea (9)
Omagh Integrated Primary School

DIFFERENCES

When people are different they don't agree.
It means you don't think the same way as me.
If they could just stop and think of life as a game,
And beneath the skin we are all the same.

Gavin Scott (9)
Omagh Integrated Primary School

LONELINESS

Loneliness is black, for there is only one shade
It tastes like a single cornflake
A sweet took out of a pile
A single grain of sugar.

It smells like
The dullness of an empty room
A book with no writing
Air running through the sky.

It looks like nobody's there for you
A tree in the middle of a field
A garden with nothing there.

It sounds like nobody's voice
A dog without a bark
A world with no sound.

It feels like an empty heart
A touch of desert
A deserted island.

It makes me wonder if anyone's out there.

Steven McCusker (9)
Omagh Integrated Primary School

HAPPINESS

Happiness is yellow
It tastes like candy sweets and fizzy pop
It smells like an air freshener always following you
It looks like flowers on a sunny day
It sounds like birds singing a song
Happiness is a joke which always makes me giggle.

Melissa Smith (10)
Omagh Integrated Primary School

FEAR

Fear is sloppy green
It tastes like a raw lemon
It smells like a tyre bonfire
It looks like the world blowing up
It sounds like scraping claws on a blackboard
It feels like a huge slit in my finger.

Josiah Whitworth (10)
Omagh Integrated Primary School

LONELINESS

The colour of loneliness is dark green and blue,
The taste of loneliness is flavourless chewing gum,
The smell of loneliness is old smoke and ash,
The sight of loneliness is an empty back yard,
The sound of loneliness is the whistling of the wind,
The feeling of loneliness is like you are unwanted.

Patrick Grant (10)
Omagh Integrated Primary School

DIFFERENCES

My mum is sick of cooking
But I am still well fed.

My sister uses shampoo
But my hair is full of gel.

I think I can be crazy
But my sister is always calm.

I think that snow is cool
But when the sun is shining I like the swimming pool.

I am inside staying dry
While Rebecca is out getting wet.

I like this poem
But my sister is upset.

Ieuan Maguire (9)
Omagh Integrated Primary School

MY HAIR STYLE

My hair is brown, I keep it short.
My hair is black, it's down my back.
My hair is green, I keep it clean.
My hair is grey, I am old today.
When it rains my hair complains.
When it's sunny I look like a bunny.
When it's windy I look like Cindy.
When it snows I do a pose.
I like my hair when it's fair.

Paul McCrystal (8)
Omagh Integrated Primary School

BIG SANDWICH

I would love a big sandwich
I will put . . .
Jam, ham,
Pink custard, green mustard,
Nocho cheese, lovely peas,
Eggs and chicken legs,
Belfast beef, Milltown meat,
And lots more ham and jam.
Now I need two giant bits of bread.

Paul Campbell (10)
Omagh Integrated Primary School

MY MOUTH

I like my mouth,
It smiles a smile.
It gobbles my food,
It whispers lots of secrets.
My mouth sucks lollies
And licks ice cream.
I use it for singing,
I use it to scream.
My mouth can be dry,
My mouth can be wet.
Inside my tongue
And my teeth all set.
I need my mouth for eating,
I need my mouth to talk.
I need my mouth
For many things,
I love my mouth a lot.

Sarah Crawford (8)
Omagh Integrated Primary School

HIDDEN TREASURES HAIKUS

Treasures in the sea
Treasure could be anything
It might make me rich

Sharks are guarding it
Buoys are floating above me
All the fish look cool

It could be trainers
It might be lots of money
I hope it is gold

Treasures in my heart
The treasures could be my friends
It's my family.

Fearghal McMahon (9)
Roscavey Primary School

HIDDEN TREASURES

As I walk along the shiny sand
There are footsteps leading me
To a desert island.
Treasures to behold.
Jewels sparkly, shiny, glittery gold
Everything is light.
No dark colours can I see,
But the loveliest treasures of all
Are my treasured fabulous friends.

Antonnia Susan Reid (9)
Roscavey Primary School

HIDDEN TREASURES

Delicate flower
Growing under the white snow
Spring is beginning.

Patrick Donnelly (9)
Roscavey Primary School

HIDDEN TREASURES

At the bottom of the sea,
The fish swim with glee,
Around a treasure chest,
They see coins of gold,
Some new, some old,
Shining at their best,
I swim down to see,
What is there for me,
In the treasure chest.

Shauneen Smyth (9)
Roscavey Primary School

HIDDEN TREASURES

Treasures everywhere
Hard to find, it must be there
Is it over there?

It could be flowers
Maybe some extra hours
Or magic powers

It could be my friends
Who will love me to the end
Thank you God for them.

Roisin McSorley (10)
Roscavey Primary School

HIDDEN TREASURES

Once I was shy.
Didn't have any confidence.
Had no feelings at all.
Then I went
Deep, deep inside myself.
I found the greatest treasure of all.
My confidence,
Feelings,
And I wasn't shy anymore.
This was everything I ever wanted
And more.

Caroline McNelis (8)
Roscavey Primary School

HIDDEN TREASURE

I have a hidden treasure
It's very special to me
It's not a rock, it's not a box
But it's something inside of me
It makes my life so special
I treasure it the most

It's like a mum
It's like a friend
It's the thing I treasure most
It's so secure, it's so supreme
It's like a special buddy
Well my special buddy is my feelings
That keep me safe and I love it.

Samone Ann Reid (11)
Roscavey Primary School

Hidden Treasure

I hid some treasure
Down by the sea
I put it in a metal box
That keeps it safe for me

I lost my treasure
Down by the sea
I wish I had it
Back here with me

I found my treasure
Down by the sea
I looked at it
It looked at me

I'll tell you what my treasure is
My *feelings*
The most special part of me.

Kerrie McNelis (11)
Roscavey Primary School

HIDDEN TREASURES

You find treasures anywhere
In your slippers
Up the stairs
You find treasures anywhere
But the greatest treasure you can find
In your heart
That's why you are loving and kind.

Michelle Woods (11)
Roscavey Primary School

HIDDEN TREASURES

I wonder where the treasures are,
I know I'll find them soon.
Through tough times and easy times,
I'm sure they'll help me soon.

In the deep, cold ocean,
The troubles start to arrive.
I feed the sharks biting my toes,
But I know I can't stop now.

I feel the soft sand curled around my feet,
The birds are singing with pride.
It feels like heaven,
But something tells me I have to stop.

A hand lands softly on my shoulder,
It's a miracle, it is God,
He tells me the treasures are in my heart,
Now I know I have to stop.

Anita McSorley (8)
Roscavey Primary School

HIDDEN TREASURES

H idden treasures in the sea
I n the smallest cave
D own between two rocks
D own just enough so I can see
E verything I have is there
N ecklaces, money, lots of stuff are hidden in the sea

T reasures hidden in the sea
R ainbow colours in the chest
E verything I possess
A re hidden in my special place
S pecial things I keep in there
U nder all that salty sea
R ed, yellow, pink and blue
E ven though it is pretend
S ure now I know it will not end.

Cathy Donnelly (9)
Roscavey Primary School

SPACE ADVENTURE

Five, four, three, two, one
We are off to space
In total calm and peace
I hope to see a UFO.

I hope to find a new planet
Where I can see
What no one has ever seen before
Things people have dreamt about.

All I want is to say
I have been there
And saw a UFO.

Michael Lynn (10)
St Colmcille's Primary School

BAD HAIR DAY!

When my hair is quite bad
I get called the lad!

When my hair is in curls
I get called *Curly.*

When my hair is in a mess
They picture me in a dress!

When my hair is in waves
I think I need shock waves!

Cathal Byrne (11)
St Colmcille's Primary School

LITTLE BROTHERS ARE FREAKS!

When I feed them their dinner
They seem to get thinner!
When I send them to their room
They beat me with a broom!
He wakes me when I'm snoring
Saying, 'Look out the window, it's pouring!'
That's some of the story of my little bro
I'll come back later for another go!

Ryan McBride (10)
St Colmcille's Primary School

KNIGHT

If you were me
You'd have a sore knee
Because I was in a fight
With a knight!

I fought with all my might
It was a really hard fight
Finally it ended
Now it's time to go get mended.

Martin Lilly (10)
St Colmcille's Primary School

FOOD

What's that on the cooker in the kitchen?
By any chance is it chicken?
Chips or sweet and sour?
Is it something I will devour?

What's that in the oven?
Is it something I'll be loving?
Is it bread or cake?
Is it something you can bake?

What's that in the bin?
Rotten leftovers
What a sin.
That's the last time I'll look in!

John Maguire (10)
St Colmcille's Primary School

SILENT SENTINELS OF THE NIGHT

The silent sentinels of the night,
Standing tall in all their might,
Plain in view and plain in sight,
Looking down from their great height.

Pure dead stone,
Black and cold,
Carved in likeness
Of life.

Of famous person,
Of animal,
Of anything at all,
These figures stand
Proud and tall,
Images of them all.

From wood or rock
Embedded in the ground
These carved figures
Can be found.

Justin Blanchard (10)
St Colmcille's Primary School

THE FLEAS!

The black death is here
And is very severe
People are dying around
Not even knowing how it's lost or found!

But it's the ships
Coming to dock in
The rats get off
And jump in the bin.

But the thing is
It's not really the rats
It's them darn old fleas
That cause the disease.

Doctors, oh doctors
You haven't got a clue
Most of you are dying
Because of the flu!

Joseph McDermott (10)
St Colmcille's Primary School

I HATE MY TEACHER

I hate my teacher
She thinks she's the boss!
All the time she is really cross
I hate her because she gives us work
She really is a great big jerk!
I think she is a silly bat
I'd like to feed her to a giant rat!

I hate my teacher
She thinks she is cool
I'd like to throw her into a swimming pool
People say she's not that bad
But personally I think she's
Stark raving mad!

I hate my teacher
She smells like a toad
I wish she'd get run over on the road
My teacher is a great big fool
I wish they'd fire her from the school!

Ryan Hackett (11)
St Colmcille's Primary School

ROMANTIC

The first time I saw you
I thought you were sweet
Then I asked you to meet me
But you were quite a cheat.

She said she was too good for me
But the real reason was
She was going with someone
Called Lee!

So I left her alone but I began to moan
So I got the phone book and lifted the hook
But all she said was
'Leave your message after the tone.'

I went to her house and I heard a cry
For she had seen a mouse
So I went to rescue her
But I came out with a sight
She didn't want me there.

So I left her house
But I was determined to have her
So I bought her a fur coat
Then she gave me a kiss
And I said that I would miss her
For she was leaving.

But I followed her car
So when she stopped
I gave her a Mars bar
And she said I was sweet
And her I could meet.

Of course like any normal person
I said, 'Yes!'

Rory Breslin (11)
St Colmcille's Primary School

WHEN I FEEL SAFE

I feel safe in my bed
Thinking, oh boy, I'm glad I am not out
There with the rain tapping on my window
The wind howling
Beware! I hear the tree leaves rustling
The gate slam closed
I cuddle up in my blankets
And curl up my toes
I pull the blanket over my nose
My eyes just appear
Then I go to sleep
My heart full of fear.

Richard Chism (11)
St Colmcille's Primary School

THE GIRL FOR ME

The girl for me
Was very wee
She was only
Four foot three!

She'd long black hair
And loved the fair
As if I could care!

Conor Madden (11)
St Colmcille's Primary School

THE TIGER

What do I see?
Oh dear me!
I see a big orange body
Which looks like honey
He has big stripes
Like black currants ripe
His eyes are big
Bigger than sticks
His teeth are as sharp as knives
Just like his wives
What do I see?
A tiger just like me!

Ciaran O'Doherty (10)
St Colmcille's Primary School

YOU'RE . . .

You are a dude
You're not naughty or crude
And you're usually very good
You make us laugh
You make us cry
But only when you tell a lie
All together you're lots of fun
I really think you're number one!

Peter Harte (11)
St Colmcille's Primary School

SCHOOL

I hate getting up for school,
I'd rather go to the pool.
In class we work so hard all day,
While in the pool we laugh and play.

When break time comes we go out to play,
And that's the best time of the day,
But when the bell sounds we head for class,
We can't wait for the day to pass.

Thank God school is over,
Now I'm home at last
Free to watch TV
School work's in the past!

Michael Sharkey (11)
St Colmcille's Primary School

MY MOTHER

She loved me
She cared for me
She made me laugh
She helped me take a bath
When I went to bed
She put the pillow under my head.

Aine Maguire (10)
St Macartan's Primary School

WITCH SPELL

One night I had a fright behind the ditch
With a witch
She got up
She caught a frog, toad, spider and a woodlouse
She flew into her cottage
She made a spell in a big pot
That's the old ragged witch.

Cathan McCourt (10)
St Macartan's Primary School

THE SPELL FROM HELL ON HALLOWE'EN NIGHT

A frog's heart
A lizard's stomach
A sheep's brain
A cow's liver
Throw them in the river
With a monkey's tail
Invite the farmer down, he'll bring a round bale!
Throw it in the river
Make the farmer shiver
Stir it all up
Then you see a pup
It starts drinking the potion
Along with sun tan lotion
The puppy dies
Along come some flies
They start eating the puppy
What a sight!
Hallowe'en night, certainly gives me a fright!

Ciaran Slevin (10)
St Macartan's Primary School

THE SPELL

A sprinkle of eyes
Followed by flies
Then a wolf's leg
Followed by a peg
Don't forget the teeth
Then a bit of beef
Bring in the nails
And a monkey's tail
Last but not least
Is a very crabbit beast.

Sean Curran (10)
St Macartan's Primary School

MY POEM

I know a man called Mr Blue, he wears a beanbag on his shoe
I know a man called Mr Red, he has a friend called Mr Ted
I know a man called Mr Purple, he has a pet gerbil
I know a man called Mr Black, he is old and has a bad back
I know a man called Mr White, he is on his way to his flight
I know a man called Mr Yellow and when he eats his stomach bellows
I know a man called Mr Green and he doesn't like too many beans.

Donna McManus (9)
St Mary's Primary School

I LOVE TO DO MY HOMEWORK

I love to do homework,
It makes me feel so great,
My mum sometimes helps me,
So my dinner is sometimes late.

I love to do my homework,
When I go to bed,
The only problem is,
I break my pencil lead.

I love to do my homework,
My favourite subject maths,
I am sad when it's all done,
So I go and have a bath.

I love to do my homework,
But I am glad when it is done,
So I can spend some time,
Having loads and loads of fun.

Lauren McRory (9)
St Mary's Primary School

HOMEWORK

I love to do my homework
I do it every day,
I do it till I play outside
Then I come in to stay.
It is sometimes quite hard
Well so my friends do say,
They are really good friends
We will stay together for eternity.
I love to do my homework
And I hope you do too.

Sarah Murray (9)
St Mary's Primary School

BUNNY RABBIT

I saw a lovely bunny rabbit
It was white and cuddly too.
I never saw a bunny rabbit
As cuddly as you.

I saw a cute bunny rabbit
As happy as can be,
Eating carrots all day long
Sitting on my knee.

I saw a funny bunny rabbit
Hopping on the path,
Then I saw him running and
Jumping, cutting the path in half.

I saw a silly bunny rabbit
Doing magic tricks.
The magic tricks that he was doing
Was messing with some sticks.

Roisin Brogan (8)
St Mary's Primary School

SHAPES!

There's a square, a triangle and a circle too,
There's all kinds of 2D shapes pink and blue.
Oval, diamond and rectangle as well,
They could be orange, that would look well.

There are 3D shapes also,
Like a cube and cuboid.
They could be white or brown,
Sometimes they look like clowns.
And silly ones at that.
There are pyramids too,
To hold the mummies back.

I hope you have enjoyed our little chat,
Of 2D shapes, and all that.
It's quite relaxing, if you don't mind me saying.
Now come on the shapes are playing!

Laura Harper (9)
St Mary's Primary School

MY FLYING CAT

My flying cat is so very fat
She has two wings that can sing and they
Even sometimes go ping.
One night the cat flew away and ditched
In a garden where she had to pay.
All her money was gone,
And tomorrow she's even
Going to cut the lawn.
Oh poor old pussy cat, I wish you weren't
as fat.

Ciara McGartland (9)
St Mary's Primary School

MY AUNTIE

My auntie is from England,
She's very, very fat.
She thinks she's the best,
But big deal about that.

She's aged thirty-four,
She's ten times fatter
Than the tall fat door.

She thinks she is good,
She thinks she is cool,
She thinks she's better,
When she is at school.

Nicole Ward (10)
St Mary's Primary School

DOGS

I like dogs
Any type of dog,
even a dog that bites,
or is not too fond of me.

I like dogs,
any type of dog,
a miniature Yorkshire terrier,
all the way up to an Irish wolfhound
I mean any type of dog.

I like dogs,
any type of dog,
my nana has a dog
it's an Alsation
her name is Sheba.
My nana had two older dogs
the names were Blondy and Gypsy,
when they died I was sad.

I like dogs,
any type of dog,
up at our caravan there are two
Norwegian elkhounds.
They are nice dogs
Norwegian elkhounds are one
of my favourite types of dog.

I like dogs,
any type of dog,
dogs are my favourite type of animal
in the four-legged world.

Callum McKinney (10)
St Mary's Primary School

GOODBYE GRANDPA

When I was young just about two,
My grandpa died during the afternoon.
I was there as well and my granny was too.
We were going to the park just down the lane.

My grandpa began to sway
Then soon he dropped to the ground.
There he lay. He did not move and he did not speak.
All he did was lose his strength.

My granny rushed to the phone
I was left all alone.
About ten seconds after my granny left
He woke up a minute before death.
Out of his pocket he took his red and white handkerchief
And gave it to me.

Then Granny came rushing
But it was too late.
He had passed away.
Up until this day
I still have my grandpa's handkerchief.
Goodbye Grandpa

Ciara Kelly (10)
St Mary's Primary School

MY LOST FRIEND

I miss my old friend
even thought I have new ones.
They may even be improved ones
but I care a lot about her
and miss her.
Sometimes I think I can hear her.
Now she has left, so I feel sad.

Melissa McDonagh (10)
St Mary's Primary School

SKATEBOARDING

Every week day night
I get out my skateboard.
Boy you want to see me!
I can Ollie,
I can grind,
I can do board slides.

Andrew McDowell (10)
St Mary's Primary School

MY DREAM

My dream is to be a singer.
To sing on a stage and be
Samantha Mumba.

My dream is to be a disco dancer
And to be a star.
My dream is to be a teacher
And teach people.

My dream is to be Lisa in the Simpsons.
My dream is to be an angel and glow like a star.
My dream is to be a hairdresser and do people's hair.

Colleen Owens (9)
St Mary's Primary School

MY BROTHER

My brother is like no other.
He's very small and a lot of bother.
Sometimes I wish he would go away,
But most of the time I want him to stay.
He always bounces on my bed,
Sometimes I wish that he was dead.
He always acts like a pest
But deep down inside he will always be the *best!*

Naoise Devlin (10)
St Mary's Primary School

FOREVER FRIENDS

I've got a friend who
drives me round the bend.
She's very kind
and she speaks her own mind.

She's very important to me
just like my family.
She's very smart
and brilliant at art.

My friend is here to stay
but if she leaves I'll cry all day.
I've got a friend
who drives me round the bend.

She's very caring,
and she's always sharing.
She doesn't like school,
But of course, that's cool.

She likes playing hockey,
but she's not very cocky.
Her teeth are white
and she's ever so bright.

She's very funny
and her favourite animal is a bunny.
I've got a friend
who drives me round the bend!

Moira Fox (10)
St Mary's Primary School

SCHOOL

School can be cool
But sometimes I'm a fool.
All my friends like to play
Play with modelling clay.
Sometimes I think my writing is neat
But other times I don't give it time.
I like maths, science, English and games.
We learn so many different things.
How to treat adults and children alike.
At school we make lots of friends.

Sinead Morris (10)
St Mary's Primary School

THINGS I LIKE TO DO

Tony Hawks likes to skate,
All around the American state.
He keeps his board in top condition,
To be like him, I'm on a mission.

Skating is the one sport for me,
I practise every day with my mate Lee.
I love to grind,
Instead of reading books that exercise my mind.

It would be great to use a ramp,
And maybe one day, go to a skating camp.
Some of this is a distant dream
But one day I will play for an international team.

Seamus Slevin (10)
St Mary's Primary School

WHAT'S GOING ON IN MY WORLD!

What's going on in *my* world,
I ask again and again.
I cry every night
For people that fight,
And pray that everyone will be all right!

What's going on in *my* world,
I ask again and again.
Well I have no granda,
But I still have my grandma.
Nothing really is the same!

What's going on in *our* world,
I ask again and again.
We should all try to love each other,
Father, mother, sister and brother.
So that we can live with one another!

What's going on in *our* world,
I ask again and again.
Why should I have so much to eat?
When there are people dying on the street!
I can't believe I have such *greed!*

What's going on in *your* world,
I really want to know.
Are you happy?
Are you sad?
I guess we will never know!

Shona McAleer (10)
St Mary's Primary School

MY LITTLE HAND

When I was born on the 19th July 1991
I was born with a little hand,
Everyone thought it was cute, but I was the only one
who didn't.

When I was only a year old,
I still had my doubts
About the little hand that God made,
That was only made for me.

When I turned four years old,
I got a letter from the postman,
It said, 'Cahir come to the hospital,
I need to look at your hand.'

When I was six years old,
I had to go to the hospital.
I was very frightened,
But my dad said it wasn't going to hurt.

When going to the theatre,
My heart was beating so fast.
I thought I'd never see my hand again,
But I knew it was going to be all right.

When coming out of theatre,
I was very, very dizzy.
Everything was going round and round,
I felt I was going to be sick.

When I wasn't dizzy,
I couldn't see my hand.
It was covered in white cloth,
Which was called a bandage.

When I got a little better,
It was time for me to go.
I thanked the nurses very much,
As it was all worthwhile.

My hand is much more free now,
I use it quite a lot.
I've now got one less finger,
But thank God for my little hand.

Cahir McKenny (10)
St Mary's Primary School

MY COUSIN BETH

My cousin Beth died,
When she was only one.
She died with a hole in her heart,
I was so sad, I only got to see her once.

I didn't even get to say goodbye,
The day she died I got a picture.
I looked at it so much I lost it.
I cried and cried so much until I got
                    my sister's picture.

I lie in bed every night,
And ask God why did she die?
I sometimes think to myself,
I want to be in Heaven with her.

She's all alone up there,
But I know she's always there.
Up in Heaven waiting for me,
To come up and join her in that peaceful place.

Samantha Munton (10)
St Mary's Primary School

MY FRIEND

My friend is always there for me,
And helps me if I cut my knee.
She isn't very bossy
Her things are always new and glossy
But she shares with me.

My friend always lets me play
And always asks me am I OK.
She's caring and gentle
And never gets down
She's really happy all year round.

My friend helps me with my maths
And never messes around in class.
She's the really friendly one,
It's my friend the one that is fun.

Amanda Hood (9)
St Peter's Primary School

FOOTBALL

Football is my
favourite subject
it gives me some
exercise and
I am very good
at football!

I kick the ball
I run so fast
back to the goalie
first and last
and when I score
I want more!

Rosaleen Bradley (9)
St Peter's Primary School

MY BROTHER

My brother wears glasses
And doesn't like lasses.
He is chatty in school
And swims in the pool.
My brother Brendan.

He is big and thin
And has lovely skin
And does like school.
He doesn't share
And doesn't care
About school!

Nuala Kelly (9)
St Peter's Primary School

MY DOG

My dog is black and white
And is very light.
My dog digs a lot,
His name is Spot.
His mum's name is Dot.

My dog has to get washed every day
I don't know I do it anyway.
He barks loudly and walks proudly,
I like my dog very much.

Mark Sharkey (9)
St Peter's Primary School

MY MUM

My mum is so bossy.
She tells me to keep my room glossy.

When I'm lying in bed
She thinks I am dead
But really, oh really I need to be fed.

She took my shopping
And all round the shops I went hopping.

She bought me a jacket,
It cost her a packet.

Carmel McBride (9)
St Peter's Primary School

MY MOBILE PHONE

My mobile phone is great
I use it every day.
I only text my friends
To keep my bill at bay.
But sometimes you have to change it
To a better phone,
When I get the new one
I bin the old one straight away.
I hope there is a place for unwanted phones,
Where they can run and play.

Adrian McBride (9)
St Peter's Primary School

SCHOOL

Why! Mum why!
School's trouble
And you know it.
Just one day off!
Walk out that door
Or there'll be more trouble!
So sadly I walked out the door.
If only there was no school
I'd be the queen of the house.
I'd buy all the sweets you could imagine.
If school was out, I'd have fun no doubt!

Ciara Furey (9)
St Peter's Primary School

MY BROTHER

My brother
we play at night.
We start to fight.
My brother
is a bother!

He shouts,
he yells
and Mum
he tells
on me.

He's loud,
he's bold,
he drives me mad,
but if anything happened him
I'd be so sad.

Denise McCullagh (9)
St Peter's Primary School

MY TEACHER

My teacher's name is Mary-Jane.
She is a nice teacher and she always helps.
If you get something wrong, she says, 'Try again!'
The rest of my class think she is OK, but I think she is
better than OK.
She scolds at times and frowns, but when she stops
scolding, she calms down.

Orla Harkin (9)
St Peter's Primary School

AMERICA

America is the best,
I know because I am from there.
You never have time to rest,
And it doesn't matter what you wear!

You can play for the whole day,
For most of the year.
Everybody is bright and gay,
And they all wear modern gear.

My favourite thing about America is,
That the fun never stops,
In LA there is showbiz,
And lots and lots of shops!

Beth Donnelly (10)
St Peter's Primary School

MY PETS

My pet is rather small,
Well I don't think he is very tall.
I went to feed him one day,
And then I saw that he had run away.

I miss him very much,
All I have left is the rabbit hutch,
I wish he hadn't run away,
Because I feel sad every day.

Now I have another pet,
When she is out she gets wet.
She is a dog black and white,
I think she is a beautiful sight.

Catherine Morris (9)
St Peter's Primary School

MY DOG

My dog called Jessy,
Is ever so messy.
She likes to chew
But it's my shoe.
She takes.
She comes to me
Every day
I think that she
Would like to say
Play with me.

Michael McCullagh (8)
St Peter's Primary School

COLOURS

Blue is for the sky and sea,
Yellow is for the sun that shines down on me.
Green is for grass and trees,
Gold is for the daffodils that blow in the breeze.
Red is for the fire burning bright.
Black is for the sky at night.
Orange is for the colour of the leaves when they fall,
Indigo is the colour of my bedroom wall.
Purple is for the heather on the mountain.
Brown is for the birds sitting on the top of the fountain.
Put red, orange, yellow, green, blue and indigo together
For what?

Eilis Kearney (9)
St Peter's Primary School

MY CAT

My cat is called Jasper
I bought her in Mace.
She sits on the sofa
And jumps on my face.
When she is sleeping
I feel like weeping.
But when I shout
I put her out.
Though she is a pest
I love her the best.

Mark McDermott (8)
St Peter's Primary School

MY BIG SISTER

My big sister
She's so kind and sometimes we fight at night.
We make good friends again in the morning.
She is annoying when she tells me to tidy up my room
But other than that she is really good
And does what she should.

Danielle McGaughey (9)
St Peter's Primary School

Dogs

A dog called Craig is taught to beg
And is so cute, he could play the flute.
He helps on the farm and does no harm.
He guides the sheep and does not sleep.
Till work is done.

Brendan Kelly (8)
St Peter's Primary School

PETS

Pets, pets
They all come in sets.
Pets, pets
They always have to go to the vet's.

I have a dog
That chews at a log.
She is black
As a coal sack.

I have two cats
That love a lot of pats.
They are greedy
And one is called Beady.

I have five fish
That would eat from a dish.
They like their food
But too much isn't good.

My advice is to never get a pet
Because if they die you will be upset.

Colm Hicks (10)
St Peter's Primary School

THE CONFUSING POEM

The wardrobe I got
The clothes that I bought
I fixed it and fixed it
And tossed it about.

When I looked in one day
I saw a doorway
And inside a leprechaun was standing
Unwinding it was.

The leprechaun said three wishes I have
And so I wished for two
I had one wish left
Guess what? I give it to you.

Brigid McCullagh (11)
St Peter's Primary School

MUSIC

There are different kinds of music,
Classical and pop.
There are also other kinds,
Like jazz, rap and rock.

There are different kinds of instruments,
The cello and the flute.
There are also other kinds,
Like the trumpet that goes toot.

There are different kinds of bands,
That sing different kinds of songs.
Some of them are short and
Some of them are long.

Patricia Morris (11)
St Peter's Primary School

MY NEW SCHOOL

When I was nine,
I moved to a new school,
I had to do what I was told
And obey the rules.

I remember when I walked in the gate,
I hoped that I would not be late,
I met a lot of new friends,
And their books they had to lend.

Now I'm glad that I'm here,
Every day I go to school with cheer,
People are very nice to me,
That's why I'm happy here in
St Peter's Primary.

Jamie Allen (11)
St Peter's Primary School

MY DAD'S HOBBY

My dad's hobby is working.
He does it every day.
The engines are taken apart,
And on the ground they lay.

He likes to get covered in grease and oil
And his clothes end up in a mess.
He lies on his back under a lorry.
He tells Mum that he is sorry.

Gerard McBride (9)
St Peter's Primary School

PLACES I COULD GO . . .

I wish I could go to a place far away,
A place where I didn't have to pay,
Like a ride on a cloud,
Where I could shout louder and louder.

I wish I could go to space,
And have a race,
On a mission for the president,
Who lived as a resident.

I wish I could go underwater,
In the water which goes pitter patter,
I'd see fish under the sea,
Some of them bigger than me.

But now I wish I could be at home in bed.

Niamh Murphy (10)
St Peter's Primary School

SPORT

I like football I like fun
I like to run with everyone

All those tears
All those cheers

Oh what a goal Michael Owen
Michael Owen number 1
Running up the left
Goal oh what a goal
Michael Owen scores.

Shane McBride (10)
St Peter's Primary School

FOOTBALL

Football is crazy
Football is mad
When I play football I am so glad

I like to kick football in the park
And play with my friend Marc
We kick a ball to each other
Until I am called by my mother

Football is a game I enjoy
It can be played by a girl or boy
Football helps to keep me fit
That is why it is such a hit.

Piaras Bradley (10)
St Peter's Primary School

MY HAMSTER

My hamster is a friend to me
He is like my best friend
He is called Nibbles
He is like a part of the family
I tell him things I don't dare

I have a hamster who is funny
I give him a nut sometimes
If he is good
But he is also a pest
Then I don't look after him he is the best

I like him very much
I know he is so funny
He is so comical
You would think he was a bunny.

Aine Conway (10)
St Peter's Primary School

SWIMMING

Swimming is fun.
Swimming is cool.
You swim so much that you don't want to get out.
You dive into the water and it is so cool,
But when you hear your number
You have to leave the pool.

Kevin Ward (10)
St Teresa's Primary School

FOOTBALL CRAZY

Football is fun
Football is great
Whenever it's on telly
I shout 'Go on my son.'
Football is fun
When you're even
On the pitch.
I like football
I play it every day
I like United
They're so much fun,
But whenever they lose,
I am not so happy
When they win
I stay a bit longer in bed.

Niall Donaghy (9)
St Teresa's Primary School

KITTENS

Kittens are fun
And very cute,
They cuddle up
Warm in your arms
Kittens are cute,
When they're hunting down birds
Like all kittens should,
Kittens are cute
When they are sleeping
On your sofa
But when they die
It is very sad.

Conor Donnelly (8)
St Teresa's Primary School

FOOTBALL

In football you can run
In football you can jump
In football you can dive
In football you can shout
In football you can kick
In football you can throw
In football you can reach up
In football you can solo
In football you can fist pass
In football you can exercise
In football you can warm up
In football you can change
In football.

Kellie Boyle (8)
St Teresa's Primary School

CATS

Cats are fun
Cats are cuddly
Cats are cool just like me and you
We like to cuddle them
But when it comes to clean the kitty litter
We don't like that.
They play all day and hunt the birds
When they are tired they cuddle up in your arms.
Sometimes they go to the toilet in your house
But if they are house trained they go to the back door.
They are cute but when they scratch you in your face
You don't think much of them.
I am sad when they go to bed in their house.

Peter Grugan (10)
St Teresa's Primary School

STYLE!

Style is long trousers
With a body top.
Style is for me and you
So let's go and shop.
Look at the sandals
And all the cool shoes.
They better be high
Or it's not style.

Style is red lipstick
With red hair mascara too,
Put on cherry lip gloss
And you'll look so cool.
You need a nice hairstyle
To go with your looks.
Try not to hide your makeup
When you're reading books.

Style is fancy belts
With classy patterns on them,
Go into the town to find them
And remember to be more than one of them.
Style!

Niamh McElduff (9)
St Teresa's Primary School

TELEVISION

I'm watching TV.
Hooray for me.
I'm lying on the seat.
I'm drinking coke and eating crisps.
I won't leave a single bit.

Scooby Doo and Flintstones too.
Time is really flying.
Oh not again,
My younger sister is already crying.
Turn to the pop channel.
Oh yes it's Westlife singing.
I can't hear the TV
Because the phone is ringing.
Yes! Daddy's off now.
No! It's time for bed.
My face has gone bright red.

Mairéad Kelly (9)
St Teresa's Primary School

UNDER THE SEA

Waves roar
And slam the shore
To seek the unknown,
Find the treasure and row home.
It could be in an undersea tomb,
Pollution in the sea is like a bomb.
All the fish and sharks with new barks
And pretty bubbles they blow.
Down in the sea high or low,
Under the sea there's no reason to moan.
Down by the seaside
Where you'll dive and float and swim and glide,
Jumping over waves,
The lifeguard saves,
Us all.

Bronagh McAteer (9)
St Teresa's Primary School

THE HAUNTED HOUSE

The haunted house
Gives me the shivers
The haunted house
Gives me the creeps
It's not really the house that's scary
It's the noise at night
Sometimes it's howling
And sometimes it's dangling chains
But the thing that really scares me the most is
Sometimes I see a ghost at *night!*

Ryan Donaghy (8)
St Teresa's Primary School

HIKING!

Get gear
For the trip.
Don't forget
The food as well.
Get your
Walking poles
And boots.
Try a high
Mountain like
Slieve Donard
Or Carrauntoohil.
So have a great hike!

Meadhbh O'Goan (9)
St Teresa's Primary School

THE STEPS TO NOWHERE

Some people say that
There are steps far away
That people go down and never come up.
I wonder what happened
That very day.
I wonder what happened to make them stay.
But never try to go down there,
Or you will get a big scare,
Because these stairs could go on forever
And never stop.
No matter what you say
I'm going there some day.

Maire Gallagher (9)
St Teresa's Primary School

DIVA STARS

Diva stars are bossy.
Diva stars are glossy.
Diva stars are fun,
But they can't run.
I like Diva stars a lot
Dive stars are very hot.
Diva stars are into fashion.
It is their biggest passion.
You have to do their hair.
It's not fair,
But I love my Diva star anyway.

Aoife McElduff (9)
St Teresa's Primary School

THE SWIMMING POOL

I like going to the swimming pool
Because you can splash each other
Dive into the pool, float up and down the pool
You can jump up and down
It is really fun, the slide is class
You can go flying down
But watch because you might bang your head
It is very sore when you come to the end
All the water will get into your eyes
It is sore
You can laugh and laugh
It was my best day at the swimming pool
I will go back some other day
Well I hope so.

Clodagh Donaghy (8)
St Teresa's Primary School

MAKE-UP

Make-up is bright
It looks good on me
Everyone will look
And they will surely see
Lip glosses and lipstick
Shining on my lips.
My mum always says
I've far too much.
Eye shadow looks good
But not too much
Because it might
Destroy the brush.
But after all it's make-up.

Sorcha Kelly (9)
St Teresa's Primary School

THE SEASONS

In spring plants begin to grow
And the animals wake up.
There is no more snow,
There is lots of new life.

In summer the sun shines a lot
And when I play games outside,
I get very hot.
I like to go to the beach.

In autumn the weather gets colder,
The leaves fall off the trees
And make a rustling sound.
Autumn is a very colourful season.

In winter it is frosty and it snows,
No plants grow.
One thing I like is Christmas day,
When I can open all my presents.

Helen Conway (11)
St Teresa's Primary School

THE THINGS THAT I HATE

Maths is the thing
that I really hate
One thing's for sure
it's not so great.

It really gets on my nerves
sometimes
I'd rather eat
a box of slime.

I really hate maths
I do, I do
This is why
I'm sitting in this goo.

Gráinne Moxon (11)
St Teresa's Primary School

BOXING CHAMPION

If you started boxing you will need
Gloves and gum shields
If you were hit without gum shields
You would lose a tooth or two

When you're in the ring it's hard work
And when you hit really hard
It's like you're hit by a lorry
Coming at full speed.

But when you get really good in the ring
You've got to hit them with all your might
And they think we're hit by lightning
Then when the ref counts to ten
You're the champion.

Finbarr McElhatton (11)
St Teresa's Primary School

BIRTHDAYS

My birthday is all about me,
all my friends here,
such a great place
to be.

Red balloons, blue balloons
yellow and green,
the coolest colours
ever seen.

Party poppers fizzy juice
all different things,
lots of presents
big and small everyone brings.

Every time December comes
I feel such joy
because it's my birthday
boy, oh boy.

Noelle Kelly (11)
St Teresa's Primary School

PLAYSTATION 2

PlayStations are good
They get you in the mood
Get a game like a frame
Put it in, what a game!
PlayStations are cool
They're not like wool
I've got a game that goes in
It can put CDs and DVDs in
I play it from 5.00pm to 6.00pm
PlayStations are cool
Even like Liverpool.

Declan Grimes (8)
St Teresa's Primary School

SHOPPING IS FUN

Shopping is fun
Shopping is great
Whenever you get something
I am as light as the sun
I go shopping
with my mate
I go popping
with the fun
Kites, lights
all things nice
When I am out
shopping I see
a lot of sights
Shopping, shopping
makes you tired
admiring all those
lovely things.

Emily Donaghy (9)
St Teresa's Primary School

CATCHING FISH

I like to catch a very big pike
Catch pike, pike, pike
The biggest pike in the world
I would even like to catch a big, big trout
Then at the end of the day
I put my fishing stuff away
No more fishing at the end of the day
I'll bring it out another day.

Niall McKernan (9)
St Teresa's Primary School

FASHION

Fashion is great
I always wear it
Trousers and T-shirt
Shoes and cool tops
Fashion is for me and you
Nobody else
Let's go and shop
Everybody wants to shop
Until the shop is empty
Fashion is lip gloss and high sandals
Hair styles with clips
That will look good on you.

Donna Grimes (9)
St Teresa's Primary School

FOOTBALL

Football is deadly, football is great
Playing football
Watching football on TV
I don't care
I stare at the TV waiting for them to score
But then it's only a game.

Conall Daly (8)
St Teresa's Primary School

OLD FRIENDS, NEW FRIENDS

I had a very good friend
One day a new girl came and took her away
My old friend said, 'Come sit with us'
I stuck out my tongue
And gave her a funny look.

At break time I said
'Come play my game'
She said, 'Sorry, I'm playing with Jane'
This time I got really mad
I tore up her book and made her sad.

I asked my old friend
'Do you want to be friends?'
She said, 'Yes!'
Now we're best friends again.

Caryn Ward (10)
St Teresa's Primary School

FRIENDS

Marian's my friend, my companion,
Through good times and bad,
My friend, my buddy through happy times and sad,
Beside me you stand, beside me you walk,
You're there to listen, you're there to talk.

You come to my house,
You stay overnight,
And when we wake up,
What a beautiful sight,
The sun is so bright.

We go out and play,
We go to the park,
And then we say,
We'll always be friends,
With happiness,
With smiles,
With pain and tears,
I know you'll be there throughout the years.

Paula Kelly (11)
St Teresa's Primary School

MY DREAM

Zzzz
One day I'll be a hero
Like Petrov and win the Scottish Cup
And the score is 2-0.

I came out of the changing rooms
I was speechless and ran out
The ref blew the whistle for kick-off
And the ball came to me
I got tackled but it was a free kick
Yes! Top corner
Suddenly my brother was shouting in my ear
'Get up,' he said, 'you'll be late for school'
And that was the end of Petrov and my career.

Aidan McCullagh (11)
St Teresa's Primary School

FASHION!

In the year 2002
All the fashion's like
Flared trousers
Belly tops
High heeled shoes
Short skirts
Lipstick
Lip liner
But grown-ups don't know
What fashion is
I'll soon show them
Groovy slippers
Hipsters
Perfume
And bright suits
Models wear fashion on the catwalk
All models like to talk about is
Fashion, fashion, fashion.

Fashion is cool
Not like school.

Orla McCartan (10)
St Teresa's Primary School

GREAT GRANNY MCCRYSTAL

Great Granny McCrystal,
I miss her so much,
It's nearly five years since
I've felt her touch.

Her chubby red cheeks
And her lovely blue eyes,
Her face so kind
And her smile so wide.

She sat in her wheelchair
All day long,
Beside the fire,
Burning so strong.

In my memory,
She will stay,
Forever and ever,
Each day!

Ciara McElduff (10)
St Teresa's Primary School

WRESTLING

W is for winning
R is for rough
E is for enjoyment
S is for Smackdown
T is for titles
L is for loud noises
I   is for introduction
N is for new wrestlers
G is for glory.

Sean McDermott (11)
St Teresa's Primary School